I0492607

LIMITLESS LEADERSHIP

Peter Amenkhienan

Copyright © 2019 PETER AMENKHIENAN

LIMITLESS LEADERSHIP

ISBN: 9798718683899

All rights reserved. No part of this publication may be reproduced, stored in a retrieval system in any form or by any means electronic, mechanical, photocopying, recording or otherwise without prior permission. Unless otherwise indicated, all scripture quotations are taken from the King James Version.

For Information Address: For further information, Enquiries, Permission Please contact E-mail: faithamenkhienan@gmail.com

Contents

INTRODUCTION

L eadership alights on the shoulders, not of those who desire to lord it over others but on those who assume the responsibility of doing whatever is necessary to get a job done. It lies on those who respond quickly to serve, those who want to help others get to where they want to go, and those who dream of beating the odds and achieving the dream.

"For the kingdom of heaven is as a man travelling into a far country, who called his own servants, and delivered unto them his goods. And unto one he gave five talents, to another two, and to another one; to every man according to his several ability; and straightway took his journey.

Then he that had received the five talents went and traded with the same, and made them other five talents. And likewise he that had received two, he also gained other two. But he that had received one went and digged in the earth, and hid his lord's money.

After a long time the lord of those servants cometh, and reckoneth with them. And so he that had received five talents came and brought other five talents, saying, Lord, thou deliveredst unto me five talents: behold, I have gained beside them five talents more.

His lord said unto him, Well done, thou good and faithful servant: thou hast been faithful over a few things, I will make thee ruler over many things: enter thou into the joy of thy lord. He also that had received two talents came and said, Lord, thou deliveredst unto me two talents: behold, I have gained two other talents beside them.

His lord said unto him, Well done, good and faithful servant; thou hast been faithful over a few things, I will make thee ruler over many things: enter thou into the joy of thy lord. Then he which had received the one talent came and said, Lord, I knew thee that thou art an hard man, reaping where thou hast not sown, and gathering where thou hast not strawed: And I was afraid, and went and hid thy talent in the earth: lo, there thou hast that is thine.

His lord answered and said unto him, Thou wicked and slothful servant, thou knewest that I reap where I sowed not, and gather where I have not strawed: Thou oughtest therefore to have put my money to the exchangers, and then at my coming I should have received mine own with usury. Take therefore the talent from him, and give it unto him which hath ten talents. For unto every one that hath shall be given, and he shall have abundance: but from him that hath not shall be taken away even that which he hath. And cast ye the unprofitable servant into outer darkness: there shall be weeping and gnashing of teeth." Matthew 25:14 - 30

This is what is lacking and in great need in Africa – a continent naturally endowed with both human and natural resources more than any other.

Leadership –that awesome phenomenon is what we need today to annex our resources together, add value to our natural endowment and thereby improve the living standards of our people. This is a great need in the government, corporate organizations, church, business entities and indeed families' particularly in Africa. Where good leaders are few, mediocre take the driving seat – a punishment for the qualified few who refuse to rise up to the challenge of leadership.

Great leaders are world changers. They are dissatisfied people, always desiring a better world and a better way of doing things. This is the only significant reason for the difference in living standards between the first world and most of the third world.

Singapore now arguably one of the most beautiful city in the world definitely owes her dramatic transformation to the great and strong leadership quality of one of her founding fathers, Lee Kuan Yew. Singapore, a Malaysian suburb till 1965, was easily granted independence because no one thought they had any significant worth.

Today, they rank among the first world countries. Lee Kuan Yew in his book, "From Third world To First World" said, "I write this book for a younger generation of Singaporeans who take stability, growth and prosperity for granted. I want them to know how difficult it was for a small country of 640 sqkm with no natural resources to survive in the midst of larger and stronger economies".

Nigeria, a country of over 200 million hard working people and far blessed in natural resources than many first world countries is also determined for transformation.

Leaders are ordinary people who accept or are placed under extraordinary circumstances that bring forth their latent potential, producing a character that inspires the confidence and trust of others. Our world today is in desperate need of such individuals.

VIEWS ON LEADERSHIP

There is a significant difference between "leadership" and "the leader". The leader is the designated position and the individual assuming the position, accepting the responsibility and accountability that accompany the designated position.

Leadership, on the other hand, is the function of the designated position and the exercise of the responsibilities involved in the position. There are many instances where individuals who are designated and placed in position as leaders fail to function and provide leadership. A title and position do not guarantee performance and productivity.

HERE ARE A FEW VIEWS ON LEADERSHIP:

☐ "Leadership is the willingness to put oneself at risk;
☐ Leadership is the passion to make a difference with others;
☐ Leadership is being dissatisfied with the current reality;

☐ Leadership is taking responsibility while others are making excuses;

☐ Leadership is seeing the possibilities in a situation while others are seeing the limitations;

☐ Leadership is the readiness to stand out in a crowd;

☐ Leadership is an open mind and an open heart;

☐ Leadership is the ability to submerge your ego for the sake of what is best;

☐ Leadership is evoking in others the capacity to dream;

☐ Leadership is inspiring others with a vision of what they can contribute;

☐ Leadership is the power of one harnessing the power of many;

☐ Leadership is your heart speaking to the hearts of others;

☐ Leadership is the integration of heart, head, and soul;

☐ Leadership is the capacity to care, and in caring, to liberate the ideas, energy, and capacities of others;

☐ Leadership is the dream made reality;

Leadership is, above all, courageous" - John C. Maxwell

"Leadership is the discipline of deliberately exerting special influence within a group to move it towards goals of beneficial performance that fulfill the group's real needs" – John Haggai

"Leadership is knowing what to do next; knowing why that's important; and knowing how to bring appropriate resources to bear on the need at hand" – Bobb Biehl

"Leadership is the ability to obtain followers" – James C. Georges

"Leadership is influence-nothing more, nothing less" – John C. Maxwell

"Leadership is the capacity to influence others through inspiration motivated by a passion, generated by a vision, produced by a conviction, ignited by a purpose" – Myles Munroe

PURPOSE OF LEADERSHIP

Where purpose is not known, abuse is inevitable and precious time, energy and resources are wasted. Leadership as a phenomenon has its primary purpose, the understanding of which will lead to successful and effective leadership in all its ramifications.

The maintenance of followers or subordinates is not the goal of leadership. Many in leadership positions today believe that their leadership should be measured by how many people look to or depend on them. This is not the purpose of true leadership.

THE ULTIMATE PURPOSE OF LEADERSHIP IS:

1. Motivation or inspiration of followers in reaching their goals, maximizing their potentials and fulfilling their purpose;
2. Mentoring of followers into becoming leaders;
3. Multiplying of leaders.

You are a successful leader when your followers have been inspired to reach their full potential and they can lead others.

True leadership brings followers into leadership. Its joy is to see others stand in their own integrity and strength, maximizing their potential in God and fulfilling the capacity of their leadership potential. This is the purpose of leadership.

The true leader measures his success and effectiveness by the diminishing degree of the dependency of his followers. Leadership has its purpose in inspiring others to exercise their leadership capacity.

LIMITLESS

"Jesus said unto him, if thou canst believe, ALL things are POSSIBLE to him that believeth" Mark 9:23

It is unarguably known and accepted truth that the Almighty God is limitless in power, possibilities, and presence. However, at creation, man was created and fashioned with limitless abilities and potential as a replica and image of divinity here on earth. You were created limitless and there is nothing that you cannot achieve.

Every man or leader who is self-aware and conscious of the inherent divine nature in him can engage the relevant forces and dynamics to become limitless in performance, productivity and possibilities.

There are no limits to what you can accomplish or to the heights that you can attain in life and in leadership except for the limits you place on yourself. Limitations live only in our minds and methodologies but if we use the power available to us as true sons and daughters of God through our God inspired imaginations, our possibilities become limitless.

"Now unto him that is able to do exceeding abundantly above all that we ask or think, according to the power that worketh in us" Ephesians 3:20

Dare to be a possibility person in thoughts and attitude. Believe in the ability of God through you to achieve great things for your life and for the kingdom. The more you believe and trust God, the more limitless your possibilities and performance in life and in leadership becomes.

I challenge you to stretch your mind, widen the frontiers of your imagination; and engage the vital principles that makes for a limitless, irresistible leadership in your sphere of in uence and you shall indeed be a LIMITLESS, IRRESISTIBLE LEADER!

WHAT IS LEADERSHIP?
Leadership is the capacity to in uence others through inspiration motivated by a passion, generated by a vision, produced by a conviction, ignited by a purpose.

TWO CARDINAL RULES
1. If you are going to lead make sure you know where you are going.
2. If you are following make sure you follow someone who knows where he is going.

CHARACTERISTICS OF GREAT LEADERS
"For David, after he had served his own generation by the will of God, fell on sleep, and was laid unto his fathers, and saw corruption:" Acts 13:36;
1. They Perceive A Need
2. They Possess A Gift.
"A man's gift maketh room for him, and bringeth him before great men." Prov. 18:16

The gift is always from God. Deborah had a natural gift/talent of strategy. Samson had a spiritual gift. Gideon and Jephthah had an acquired skill. So you need to: DISCOVER, DEVELOP, DEPLOY, and BE DISTINGUISHED by your gift.

☐ Good leaders develop and groom their gifts.
☐ They use their gift to positively impact society.
☐ The gift provides a platform for influence and you flourish because of the gift.

3. They Parade A Passion.

Know ye not that they which run in a race run all, but one receiveth the prize? So run, that ye may obtain. And every man that striveth for the mastery is temperate in all things. Now they do it to obtain a corruptible crown; but we an incorruptible. I therefore so run, not as uncertainly; so fight I, not as one that beateth the air: But I keep under my body, and bring it into subjection: lest that by any means, when I have preached to others, I myself should be a castaway. 1 Cor 9:24-27

A PASSION TO ACHIEVE. 1 Cor 9:24-27
☐ Shown in determination. 1 Cor 9:24
☐ Shown in diligence
☐ Shown in direction. 1 Cor 9:26; Matt 14:29-30
☐ Shown in discipline. 1 Cor 9:25,27
☐ Shown in dedication. Luke 9:62; 2 Tim 4:7

4. They Prepare The People.

"And Joshua said unto the people, Sanctify yourselves: for to morrow the LORD will do wonders among you. And Joshua spake unto the priests, saying, Take up the ark of the covenant, and pass over before the people. And they took up the ark of the covenant, and went before the people. And the LORD said unto Joshua, This day will I begin to magnify thee in the sight of all Israel, that they may know that, as I was with Moses, so I will be with thee." Josh 3:5-7

5. They Persuade The People.

"And Caleb stilled the people before Moses, and said, Let us go up at once, and possess it; for we are well able to overcome it." Num 13:30.

Examples are Deborah, Barak, Gideon, Samuel- his leadership spans two generations.

To persuade people you need to know the proven practices that got things done:

a. What gets talked about gets done.
b. What gets trained for gets done.
c. What gets measured gets done.
d. What gets rewarded gets done

6. They Possess A Picture Of The Future: VISION

A. Position Is No Accident - Regardless of your position in life, whether at church, at work, at school, at home, etc., you need to know that it is no accident! God has placed you where He has for a purpose. He has place you where you are for His purpose! There are no accidents or coincidences with God! You are where you are for His glory! Esther - Esther 4:14

B. Prosperity Is No Accident - The resources you have been given are not yours by luck! They have been given to you by the providence of God to be used for His glory. Find out what He would have you do with what you have! The wise men and Joseph - Matt. 2:11-15

C. Power Is No Accident - The influence you have been given in the lives of others is no accident! God has given you the ear of others for a purpose. Allow Him to use you where you are for His glory! Nehemiah and the king; Servant girl and Naaman - 2 Kings 5:3

7. They Partner With God.
"I can do all things through Christ which strengtheneth me." Phil 4:13

8. They Pursue A Purpose:
Every leader leads because they pursue a purpose. The purpose of a leader must be: Measurable, Memorable, Mobile, and Moral.

A PURPOSE TO ACCOMPLISH. Gal 2:2, Phil 2:16.
☐ Shown in focus
☐ Shown in faithfulness
☐ Shown in fruitfulness

THE CALL OF LEADERSHIP
In spiritual leadership, there are three (3) ways a man can be appointed to an office of a leader.

1. SELF-APPOINTED LEADERSHIP: Korah (Numb. 16 & 17) - The leader takes upon himself the authority and responsibility of a spiritual office into which he has not been divinely called. The Epistle of Jude verse eleven shows that in the last days, men will rise up like Korah into positions of leadership they have not been called into.

2. MAN-APPOINTED LEADERSHIP: Saul (1 Sam. 8:1-18) – The leader is called by the authority of human vessels who are not speaking by the unction of God. This leadership is common in our society today. It is humanistic, man-centered and exalts the might and wisdom of man. It puts much reliance on man's ability, training and education. But it is only God that gives the authority and grace to succeed in leadership.

3. GOD-APPOINTED LEADERSHIP: These leaders are called God's choice, appointed and placed. They receive a specific call from God for their work. (Exod. 3:4; Exod. 31:2; 1 Sam. 3:4,18; Rom. 1:1)

WHAT IS LIMITLESS LEADERSHIP?
Limitless Leadership is leadership beyond boundaries and limitations; it is leadership in any situation. It is about leaders having the ability to thrive in everything they do so that they are able to improve themselves, those around them, and everything they are involved in. Being able to lead well whether in the private, public, pew, pulpit and political arena is limitless leadership.

As you will come to understand, Limitless leadership is not about bullying, it's about believing: believing in yourself, believing in your team, believing in your goals, and most of all, believing that every tool you need to lead well is already residing within you but only needs development.

Leadership starts with our ability to lead our own lives and then transcends to our ability to positively impact the people and community around us. Limitless Leadership is leadership that endures. Limitless leadership involves the leader taking off the CONSTRAINTS or LIMITS and is achieved and enhanced through GROWING YOUR CAPACITY.

<u>GROWING</u> YOUR CAPACITY
MATT.25:14-30

"Therefore said he unto them, The harvest truly is great, but the labourers are few: pray ye therefore the Lord of the harvest, that he would send forth labourers into his harvest." LUKE 10:2

C apacity is the ability to receive or contain; the maximum amount or number that can be received or contained. Matt 25:14-30
Everyone who wants to gain more; attain new heights and achieve a higher goal than before must grow his capacity.

When you do things the same way you have been doing before, you will still have the same results. Therefore, for new results, things must be done in a new way.

It is being said that if someone is trying to solve a problem at the same level at which the problem was formed, it will be very difficult; so, one need to go higher.

In order to go into your tomorrow; into higher achievements, achieve greater feats in life, have more blessings in life, enjoy great blessings from God; you need to grow your capacity. Luke 10:2; Matt. 25:14-30

God will never give you more than you can handle. You need to check your capacity considering the level at which you are operating now. Check your capacity if you are lacking things. God is not a wicked Father or a wicked God.

God can only give you what He knows that you are capable of handling and have the ability to manage. He cannot give you what you have no ability to manage. As a good Father, God will not want to crush you or give you a load heavier than you to carry.

"Now there cried a certain woman of the wives of the sons of the prophets unto Elisha, saying, Thy servant my husband is dead; and thou knowest that thy servant did fear the LORD: and the creditor is come to take unto him my two sons to be bondmen. And Elisha said unto her, What shall I do for thee? tell me, what hast thou in the house? And she said, Thine handmaid hath not any thing in the house, save a pot of oil. Then he said, Go, borrow thee vessels abroad of all thy neighbours, even empty vessels; borrow not a few. And when thou art come in, thou shalt shut the door upon thee and upon thy sons, and shalt pour out into all those vessels, and thou shalt set aside that which is full. So she went from him, and shut the door upon her and upon her sons, who brought the vessels to her; and she poured out. And it came to pass, when the vessels were full, that she said unto her son, Bring me yet a vessel. And he said unto her, There is not a vessel more. And the oil stayed. Then she came and told the man of God. And he said, Go, sell the oil, and pay thy debt, and live thou and thy children of the rest." 2 kings 4:1-7

Increase your capacity. As long as there was capacity, there was oil to fill. As long as there is space in your capacity, God will always fill you with blessings to bless you.

"For the turning away of the simple shall slay them, and the prosperity of fools shall destroy them." Pro 1:32

"Cease not to give thanks for you, making mention of you in my prayers; That the God of our Lord Jesus Christ, the Father of glory, may give unto you the spirit of wisdom and revelation in the knowledge of him: The eyes of your understanding being enlightened; that ye may know what is the hope of his calling, and what the riches of the glory of his inheritance in the saints," Eph 1:16-18

"That he would grant you, according to the riches of his glory, to be strengthened with might by his Spirit in the inner man;" Eph 3:16 So, if you are not enjoying the good things of life, check your capacity. God will not bless or increase you beyond your capacity.

AREAS TO GROW YOUR CAPACITY.
Capacity is the ability to receive and contain.

1. GROW YOUR CHARACTER CAPACITY
What can your character handle? How many issues can you handle? Character is living clean no matter the circumstance. Doing what is right at the right time irrespective of who is watching or not. Living life on ethics rather than rules.

Character involves living a holy life. If you take care of your private life, God will take care of your public life. Take care of your character and not your activities. Character is walking your talk and talking your walk. Character is living right.

2. GROW YOUR CONTROL AND MONITORING CAPACITY. Controlling methods and motives.

3. GROW YOUR CONFIDENCE CAPACITY.
Trustworthiness or Reliability. Belief in one's Power and abilities. Confidence in God and yourself. Example - David. Believe in yourself! Have faith in your abilities. Without a reasonable con☐dence in your own powers or abilities, you cannot be a limitless leader.

4. GROW YOUR CRISIS HANDLING CAPACITY
Life is about crisis, dangers and opportunities. In every crisis, there are opportunities. Sometimes, the more the blessings, the more the crisis.

"Then Peter began to say unto him, Lo, we have left all, and have followed thee. And Jesus answered and said, Verily I say unto you, There is no man that hath left house, or brethren, or sisters, or father, or mother, or wife, or children, or lands, for my sake, and the gospel's, But he shall receive an hundredfold now in this time, houses, and brethren, and sisters, and mothers, and children, and lands, with persecutions; and in the world to come eternal life." Mark 10:28-30

5. GROW YOUR CARING AND COMPASSION CAPACITY

A person without compassion cannot care. People don't care how much you know until they know how much you care. Compassion will cure more sins than condemnation.

"Therefore, as God's chosen people, holy and dearly loved, clothe yourselves with compassion, kindness, humility, gentleness and patience." Colossians 3:12

"But when he saw the multitudes, he was moved with compassion on them, because they fainted, and were scattered abroad, as sheep having no shepherd." Matthew 9:36

6. GROW YOUR PAIN CAPACITY

The more your capacity for pain, the more your capacity for gain. You will only grow to the threshold of your pain. The difference between a big church and a small one or the C.E.O of a big firm and a small one can be the pain capacity of the leader, manager or boss.

"We are troubled on every side, yet not distressed; we are perplexed, but not in despair; Persecuted, but not forsaken; cast down, but not destroyed; Always bearing about in the body the dying of the Lord Jesus, that the life also of Jesus might be made manifest in our body." 2 Corinthians 4:8-10

7. GROW YOUR PATIENCE CAPACITY

Patience is power. It takes patience to see the promises of God fulfilled in your life. Be patient with yourself; be patient with others and be patient with life. Your capacity to be patient is the key to avoiding your greatest mistakes in life.

"That ye be not slothful, but followers of them who through faith and patience inherit the promises." Hebrews 6:12

"For ye have need of patience, that, after ye have done the will of God, ye might receive the promise." Hebrews10:36

"Wherefore seeing we also are compassed about with so great a cloud of witnesses, let us lay aside every weight, and the sin which doth so easily beset us, and let us run with patience the race that is set before us," Hebrews12:1

"But that on the good ground are they, which in an honest and good heart, having heard the word, keep it, and bring forth fruit with patience." Luke 8:15;

"In your patience possess ye your souls." Luke 21:19

"But let patience have her perfect work, that ye may be perfect and entire, wanting nothing." James 1:4

8. GROW YOUR POWER HOLDING AND HANDLING CAPACITY.

"But ye shall receive power, after that the Holy Ghost is come upon you: and ye shall be witnesses unto me both in Jerusalem, and in all Judaea, and in Samaria, and unto the uttermost part of the earth." Acts 1:8

What you do with the power given to you will determine your next level of power. When the power given to you is properly used and utilized, more power will be bestowed upon you. When Peter received the power in Acts 2:2-4, he used the power to draw three thousand souls into the kingdom (Acts 2:41) and thereafter five thousand souls (Acts 4:4), until it became multitudes of men and women from all over the city (Acts 5:14-16)

"And believers were the more added to the Lord, multitudes both of men and women.) Insomuch that they brought forth the sick into the streets, and laid them on beds and couches, that at the least the shadow of Peter passing by might overshadow some of them. There came also a multitude out of the cities round about unto Jerusalem, bringing sick folks, and them which were vexed with unclean spirits: and they were healed every one." Acts 5:14-16

What you do and how you handle your current level of power will determine your growth and increase in power. You cannot demand for more power if you have not engaged your current power level for profitable exploits.

9. GROW YOUR PRODUCTIVITY CAPACITY. Activity does not always equal productivity. Your efficiency and effectiveness as a leader is rated based on your result and output. Learn to increase your yield and productivity, no matter the resources available to you. It is productivity that decides rewards.

"Then Isaac sowed in that land, and received in the same year an hundredfold: and the LORD blessed him. And the man waxed great, and went forward, and grew until he became very great: For he had possession of flocks, and possession of herds, and great store of servants: and the Philistines envied him." Genesis 26:12-14

10. GROW YOUR PRIORITY CAPACITY.
"But seek ye first the kingdom of God, and his righteousness; and all these things shall be added unto you." Matt 6:33

Doing first things first. Doing the important first rather than the urgent first. Things which matter most must never be at the mercy of things which matter least. Your decisions reveal your priorities. What you prioritize defines your life. Let us ponder on what is truly of value in life, what gives meaning to our lives, and set our priorities on the basis of that.

11. GROW YOUR EXPOSURE CAPACITY

☐ Certain exposures can help.

☐ Increase your knowledge; learn from those who are higher than you.

☐ Learn from those who are better than you.

☐ Learn from those who have succeeded and those who are succeeding.

☐ Learn from the secrets of the great men.

LEARN AND MAKE GOOD USE OF THE FOLLOWING:

1. OPK – Other Peoples Knowledge. Learn from Other people's knowledge. Successful people attract and collect knowledge.

"And ye shall know the truth, and the truth shall make you free." John 8:32

"Through wisdom is an house builded; and by understanding it is established: And by knowledge shall the chambers be filled with all precious and pleasant riches." Prov 24:3-4

2. OPF – Other Peoples Failures. So that you will not fail where they failed. Learn what they did wrong.

"For a just man falleth seven times, and riseth up again: but the wicked shall fall into mischief." Prov 24:16

3. OPS – Other Peoples Success. Find what they are doing right. For example, the Queen of Sheba. Learn the price they paid and the process they followed.

"And the things that thou hast heard of me among many witnesses, the same commit thou to faithful men, who shall be able to teach others also." 2 Tim 2:2

4. OPI – Other Peoples Insight. Other Peoples insight will make you to have other people's ideas.

5. OPC – Other Peoples Credibility. Other Peoples credibility can move you form grass to grace; From obscurity to superiority. Let such people mentor you.

12. GROW YOUR FRIENDSHIP AND RELATIONSHIP CAPACITY
In any undertaking, one must learn to grow his relationship capacity. Learn to relate more and be friendly.

There are two kinds of people:
i. Assets – Those who deposit in your life
ii. Liabilities – Those who withdraw from your life.

☐ Having more withdrawals than deposit in life can finish you.
☐ Learn how to add value to people's life.
☐ Learn how to network because your network determines your net worth in life.
☐ Certain heights can never be achieved except God brings certain people across your way.
☐ Leave a good memory in people's life.

13. GROW YOUR SPIRITUAL CAPACITY/FAITH CAPACITY.

"For this cause I bow my knees unto the Father of our Lord Jesus

Christ, Of whom the whole family in heaven and earth is named, That he would grant you, according to the riches of his glory, to be strengthened with might by his Spirit in the inner man; That Christ may dwell in your hearts by faith; that ye, being rooted and grounded in love," Eph 3:14-17.

Learning to please God more. Doing only His will. Growing in faith.

"And he that sent me is with me: the Father hath not left me alone; for I do always those things that please him." John 8:29
God cannot give you more than you have faith to handle.

Faith is in categories:
- No Faith
"And he said unto them, Why are ye so fearful? how is it that ye have no faith?" Mark 4:40

- Weak Faith
"Him that is weak in the faith receive ye, but not to doubtful disputations." Romans 14:1

- Little Faith "And he saith unto them, Why are ye fearful, O ye of little faith? Then he arose, and rebuked the winds and the sea; and there was a great calm." Matt. 8:26

- Great Faith
"Then Jesus answered and said unto her, O woman, great is thy faith: be it unto thee even as thou wilt. And her daughter was made whole from that very hour." Matt. 15:28

14. GROW YOUR FINANCIAL CAPACITY AND FINANCE HANDLING CAPACITY. Knowing how to make, manage and multiply money.

LEARN HOW TO SECURE MONEY.

"And he said also unto his disciples, There was a certain rich man, which had a steward; and the same was accused unto him that he had wasted his goods. And he called him, and said unto him, How is it that I hear this of thee? give an account of thy stewardship; for thou mayest be no longer steward." Luke 16:1-2

God wants us to prosper. We need to learn how to make money.

1. Don't make money at the expense of life and health. "It is vain for you to rise up early, to sit up late, to eat the bread of sorrows: for so he giveth his beloved sleep." Psalm 127:2

2. Don't make money at the expense of character. "Woe unto him that giveth his neighbour drink, that puttest thy bottle to him, and makest him drunken also, that thou mayest look on their nakedness!" Habakkuk 2:15

3. Don't make money at the expense of higher values.

LEARN HOW TO SAVE MONEY.

"And the lord commended the unjust steward, because he had done wisely: for the children of this world are in their generation wiser than the children of light." Luke 16:8

1.   The Bible teaches us to save money but not to hoard it.

"Go to the ant, thou sluggard; consider her ways, and be wise: Which having no guide, overseer, or ruler, Provideth her meat in the summer, and gathereth her food in the harvest." Prov 6:6-8
"There is treasure to be desired and oil in the dwelling of the wise; but a foolish man spendeth it up." Prov. 21:20

"Go to now, ye rich men, weep and howl for your miseries that shall come upon you. Your riches are corrupted, and your garments are motheaten. Your gold and silver is cankered; and the rust of them shall be a witness against you, and shall eat your flesh as it were fire. Ye have heaped treasure together for the last days." James 5:1-3

2. The Bible is not against making money

LEARN HOW TO SPEND MONEY.

"And the lord commended the unjust steward, because he had done wisely: for the children of this world are in their generation wiser than the children of light." Luke 16:8

THINGS TO BEWARE OF WHEN SPENDING MONEY:
☐   Beware of credit buying. Prov 22:7
☐   Beware of greed and impulse buying. 1 Tim 6:8
☐   Beware of ego buying.

LEARN HOW TO SHARE MONEY.
"And I say unto you, Make to yourselves friends of the mammon of unrighteousness; that, when ye fail, they may receive you into everlasting habitations." Luke 16:9

"Honour the LORD with thy substance, and with the firstfruits of all thine increase." Prov 3:9

We need to tithe. Tithing shows our faith in God Mal 3:10. If we truly believe this verse, we will tithe. Learn to give.

"Give, and it shall be given unto you; good measure, pressed down, and shaken together, and running over, shall men give into your bosom. For with the same measure that ye mete withal it shall be measured to you again." Luke 6:38

15. GROW YOUR FAITHFULNESS CAPACITY

Many are called, few are chosen but fewer still are faithful. Faithfulness is a must if you must be trusted as a leader. Faithfulness is a vital requirement for promotion and progress in leadership. Faithfulness has a great reward as opposed to facefulness.

"His lord said unto him, Well done, thou good and faithful servant: thou hast been faithful over a few things, I will make thee ruler over many things: enter thou into the joy of thy lord. He also that had received two talents came and said, Lord, thou deliveredst unto me two talents: behold, I have gained two other talents beside them. His lord said unto him, Well done, good and faithful servant; thou hast been faithful over a few things, I will make thee ruler over many things: enter thou into the joy of thy lord." Matt. 25:21-23

"A faithful man shall abound with blessings: but he that maketh haste to be rich shall not be innocent." Prov. 28:20

16. GROW YOUR FOCUS CAPACITY.

knowing how to work all the time on high value tasks. Unsuccessful people are those who waste time each day on low value activities. Low value activities are distractions.

17. GROW YOUR RISK TAKING CAPACITY

Can you handle risk? Do you have the heart to handle risk? No risk, no rising. If you wait to be 100% sure before you take action, you are too late.

Those who have developed in the area of risk taking know how to be comfortable outside the comfort zone. They don't count losses, instead they count lessons. They know how to on challenges that lead to Championship.

18. GROW YOUR LOVE CAPACITY

Grow your love capacity for God and for man.

"And thou shalt love the LORD thy God with all thine heart, and with all thy soul, and with all thy might." Deut. 6:5.

To what extent do you love God? Can God say that you love Him with all your soul, mind, strength and heart? How do you grow your love capacity for God?

Only by keeping His commandments.

"If ye love me, keep my commandments. John 14:15.

When you keep His commandment you become a commander in life.

19. GROW YOUR VISION CAPACITY
See the big picture. Seeing well is living well. See yourself differently. See yourself as a problem solver and not in a problem.

Eyes that see are many. Vision is the art of seeing what is invisible to others. Vision is the capacity to see the possibilities of the future and create a pathway for getting there. Where there is no vision, there is no hope.

"Where there is no vision, the people perish: but he that keepeth the law, happy is he." Proverbs 29:18

20. GROW YOUR OBEDIENCE CAPACITY
"His mother saith unto the servants, Whatsoever he saith unto you, do it." John 2:5

In Luke 5:1-11, Jesus asked Peter to throw his nets (in plural) into the deep; but he threw one and caught too much. If he had thrown more than one net, he would have caught a lot more than one net could carry. He received according to his capacity. His faith was for one net according to what Jesus spoke and he had a blessing according to his faith capacity.

21. GROW YOUR GRACE CAPACITY. Increase in grace. "Grace and peace be multiplied unto you through the knowledge of God, and of Jesus our Lord," 2 Peter 1:2.

When you make use of the little grace bestowed on you, God will give you more. We are what we are by the grace of God.

22. GROW YOUR GIVING CAPACITY
Giving is living. Life and leadership is not measured in its duration but in its donation. We make a living by what we get but we make a life by what we give. Life and indeed leadership is a boomerang, what you give is what you get.

"He that believeth on the Son hath everlasting life: and he that believeth not the Son shall not see life; but the wrath of God abideth on him." Jn 3:36

"Give, and it shall be given unto you; good measure, pressed down, and shaken together, and running over, shall men give into your bosom. For with the same measure that ye mete withal it shall be measured to you again." Luke 6:38

"Every man according as he purposeth in his heart, so let him give; not grudgingly, or of necessity: for God loveth a cheerful giver. And God is able to make all grace abound toward you; that ye, always having all sufficiency in all things, may abound to every good work." 2 Cor 9:7-8

23. QUALITY THINKING CAPACITY.
Quality thinking is the platform of giant strides and accomplish-

ments as a leader. Thoughts have energy. Make sure your thoughts are positive, progressive and powerful.

Nurture your mind with good and great thoughts because you will never rise above the quality of your thoughts. Your leadership prowess is a reflection of your thinking capacity.

Finally, brethren, whatsoever things are true, whatsoever things are honest, whatsoever things are just, whatsoever things are pure, whatsoever things are lovely, whatsoever things are of good report; if there be any virtue, and if there be any praise, think on these things. Phil 4:8

24. GROW YOUR DISCIPLINE CAPACITY.

Discipline is the commitment to do what we should in a consistent way. What will close the gap between what we do and what we are capable of doing is discipline.

Everything worthwhile in life is uphill. Achieving what you want takes time, effort consistency, energy and commitment.

Self-discipline is what makes those things possible and puts success within reach. And here is the good news. Self-discipline is something you can develop. You don't need to be born with it. It is a choice you make and keep on making.

If Self-disciplines is the highway that takes us where we want to go in life, then excuses are exits off that highway. And believe me - there are a lot of exits; example, procrastination, persecution pressures, etc.

Discipline is like a muscle, the more you train it the better we become in developing it. You cannot manage your life and others if you cannot manage your time.

25. GROW YOUR TIME MANAGEMENT CAPACITY.

Limitless leaders are good time managers. They are always time conscious. They know how to maximize time by:

a.   Setting Upfront Expectations; knowing and expressing what you want to achieve.

b.   Setting external deadlines. Having schedules of activities.

THE DANGEROUS
PATHS LEADERS
SHOULD NOT TREAD
IN ORDER TO REMAIN
<u>LIMITLESS</u>

"There is a way which seemeth right unto a man, but the end thereof are the ways of death." Prov 14:12

"There is a way that seemeth right unto a man, but the end thereof are the ways of death." Prov.16:25.

L eadership is a divine, demanding and dangerous assignment. It is a place of power, privileges, possibility, probation, problems solving, purpose, productivity; a place of protocols, rules and regulations. If all these are not properly handled, the leader could be found wanting. This is why every leader must tread carefully and avoid certain paths that could limit, derail and lead to a fall.

THE DANGEROUS PATHS LEADERS SHOULD NOT TREAD.

1. The Path Of Arrogance.

"Then Uzziah was wroth, and had a censer in his hand to burn incense: and while he was wroth with the priests, the leprosy even rose up in his forehead before the priests in the house of the LORD, from beside the incense altar. And Azariah the chief priest, and all the priests, looked upon him, and, behold, he was leprous in his forehead, and they thrust him out from thence; yea, himself hasted also to go out, because the LORD had smitten him. And Uzziah the king was a leper unto the day of his death, and dwelt in a several house, being a leper; for he was cut off from the house of the LORD: and Jotham his son was over the king's house, judging the people of the land." 2 Chron 26:19-21

If you are now Arrogant and Proud because of the Success God has allowed in your life, you are in danger of falling. If you are no longer obeying divine instructions; and you are no longer giving God the Glory due to His Name as a result of your prosperity, you are in danger of losing your position and prosperity. When you find yourself in this position, you will need to Repent, Return to God and Renew your Loyalty and Commitment to Him so that you will not end up like King Uzziah.

The results of his sin was Removal, Replacement and Rejection.

2.   The Path Of Apathy *"And Samuel lay until the morning, and opened the doors of the house of the LORD. And Samuel feared to shew Eli the vision. Then Eli called Samuel, and said, Samuel, my son. And he answered, Here am I. And he said, What is the thing that the LORD hath said unto thee? I pray thee hide it not from me: God do so to thee, and more also, if thou hide any thing from me of all the things that he said unto thee. And Samuel told him every whit, and hid nothing from him. And he said, It is the LORD: let him do what seemeth him good."* 1 Sam 3:15-18.

Apathy means lack of interest in responsibilities or concern for things you are supposed to act on. It means absence or suppression of passion or emotion.

3. The Path Of Complacency.
A feeling of quiet pleasure or security, often while unaware of some potential danger, defect, or the like; self-satisfaction or smug satisfaction with an existing situation, condition, etc. Complacency will keep us from growing numerically, physically, and most of all spiritually. Convenience is great but it can be a curse for the leader who want to finish well.

4. The Path Of Compromise.
Compromise is nothing more than making a deal with someone. Giving and taking a little here and a little there. But compromise is an opponent of commitment. You see God could have comprom-

ised on the sacrifice of Jesus and "bent" the rules a little so that Jesus would not have suffered so much but then where would we be today if that was His attitude? Compromise is the adversary of total commitment to Jesus Christ.

There are no in-betweens with God. Yes, it is either black and white with God. Sin is Sin. Lying is sin no matter if it gets you off the hook. If we allow for one second compromise to be a part of our life it will be like a fast moving cancer that will within a short period time destroy us from within.

In the world in which we live in today there is no room for the spiritually weak to be able to survive. Compromise is a sure sign of spiritual weakness.

5. The Path Of Disobedience:
Saul of Benjamin started well but had a bad ending. He started in obedience but ended in disobedience. His carrier started at sunrise but ended at sunset-at night. The life of Saul is a reminder that good beginnings are no guarantee for a successful ending. Saul took 3 downward steps; 1 Sam 13:11. These are the steps of : Impatience, Unbelief and Dishonesty.

He lived on substitutes by:

A. Saying rather than Doing

"And Samuel came to Saul: and Saul said unto him, Blessed be thou of the LORD: I have performed the commandment of the LORD." 1 Sam.15:13.

But he did not perform the commandment of The Lord. It is so easy for us God's people to substitute words for action. We are supposed to be doers of the word - Not just saying the word -

"But be ye doers of the word, and not hearers only, deceiving your own

selves." James 1:22

"If we say that we have fellowship with him, and walk in darkness, we lie, and do not the truth." 1 John 1:6

B. Excuses rather than Execution
1Sam 15:15, 21 ". For the people spared the best of the sheep and of the oxen, to sacrifice unto The Lord thy God and the rest we have utterly destroyed."

Don't look for excuses to cover sins.
Prov 28:13 "he that covereth his own sin shall not prosper but he that confesseth and forsaketh them shall have mercy"

C. Sacrifice rather than Obedience
1Sam 15:22. "Behold, to obey is better than sacrifice".

Psalm 51:16-17 – "The sacrifice of God are a broken spirit and a contrite heart."

"For I desired mercy, and not sacrifice; and the knowledge of God more than burnt offerings." Hosea 6:6

D. Reputation rather than Character

"And Saul said unto Samuel, I have sinned: for I have transgressed the commandment of the LORD, and thy words: because I feared the people, and obeyed their voice. Now therefore, I pray thee, pardon my sin, and turn again with me, that I may worship the LORD. And Samuel said unto Saul, I will not return with thee: for thou hast rejected the word of the LORD, and the LORD hath rejected thee from being king over Israel. And as Samuel turned about to go away, he laid hold upon the skirt of his mantle, and it rent. And Samuel said unto him, The LORD hath rent the kingdom of Israel from thee this day, and hath given it to a neighbour of thine, that is better than thou. And also the Strength of Israel will not lie nor repent: for he is not a man, that he

should repent. Then he said, I have sinned: yet honour me now, I pray thee, before the elders of my people, and before Israel, and turn again with me, that I may worship the LORD thy God. So Samuel turned again after Saul; and Saul worshipped the LORD." 1 Sam 15:24-31.

Saul was only concerned about his reputation before the people. He was not concerned about his character or what The Lord thought about him. When you start living to please people rather than God, you will end pleasing no one including God.

There are two people named Saul in the bible, This Saul lost his crown. The Saul of Tarsus won the crown. Spiritual fall is gradual. So accept no substitutes. Read Revelation 2:4-5. They replaced intimacy with activity. Ritual above relationship. Form for fellowship. If you and I are to keep the passion burning for Christ, we can accept no substitute for intimacy with Christ.

The Reason for His Fall (in words directly from God or through Samuel): *"I regret that I have made Saul king, for he has turned back from following Me, and has not carried out My commands"* (15:11). "Why then did you not obey the voice of the LORD...?" (15:19; cf. v. 22). "For rebellion is as the sin of divination, and insubordination is as iniquity and idolatry" (15:23). "You have rejected the word of the LORD, and the LORD has rejected you from being king over Israel" (15:26).

6. The Path Of Distrust:

Distrust means lack of trust; doubt; suspicion. To regard with doubt or suspicion; have no trust in. Saul distrusted God, which led to intense jealousy and fear of David.

Much of 1 Samuel relates Saul's persecuting David. In contrast, David kept trusting God and refusing to take vengeance over Saul. This gave evidence why David was "a man after His own heart" (13:13-14).

The climax to this story was God's covenant with David: "your house and your kingdom shall endure before Me forever; your throne shall be established forever" (2 Sam. 7:16).

7. The Path Of Dishonesty.
In 1 Sam 13:11-12 King Saul blamed Samuel. In 1 Sam 14 he blamed Jonathan. In 1 Sam 15 he blamed the people. But Saul never blamed himself. Saul lost the kingdom 1 Sam 13:13-14. Later he lost the crown, and then he lost his life.

If any man had a reason to become a success it was Saul. The first king of Israel, but he flunged it. He had a divine call from God; he had the spirit of God to enable him do God's will. He had a wonderful praying prophet as a friend, ye he failed. A great failure.

8. The Path Of Evil Addiction And Evil Attraction.
"And Samson went down to Timnath, and saw a woman in Timnath of the daughters of the Philistines. And he came up, and told his father and his mother, and said, I have seen a woman in Timnath of the daughters of the Philistines: now therefore get her for me to wife. Then his father and his mother said unto him, Is there never a woman among the daughters of thy brethren, or among all my people, that thou goest to take a wife of the uncircumcised Philistines? And Samson said unto his father, Get her for me; for she pleaseth me well. Judges 14:1-3 and Judges14:4-10; 16:1-2; 4-20.

As a result of evil addiction and attraction, Samson:
☐　Lost His Vision - 16:21 - (Blind);
☐　Lost His Vitality - 16:20-21 - (Bind);
☐　Lost His Victory - 16:21 - (Grind).

He soon found out that sin has a blinding, binding and grinding effect.

9. The Path Of Greed Instead Of Generosity. 2 Kings 5:20-27
Gehazi got more than he bargained for as a result of greed.

10. The Path Of Immorality.
Immorality is a big obstacle to godliness among Christian leaders. The fall of King David should instruct us. Fill yourself with God's Word—memorize passages like

"For this is the will of God, even your sanctification, that ye should abstain from fornication: That every one of you should know how to possess his vessel in sanctification and honour; Not in the lust of concupiscence, even as the Gentiles which know not God: That no man go beyond and defraud his brother in any matter: because that the Lord is the avenger of all such, as we also have forewarned you and testified. For God hath not called us unto uncleanness, but unto holiness. He therefore that despiseth, despiseth not man, but God, who hath also given unto us his holy Spirit." 1 Thess. 4:3–8

"I made a covenant with mine eyes; why then should I think upon a maid?" Job 31:1

"Can a man take fire in his bosom, and his clothes not be burned?" Proverbs 6:27

"*But fornication, and all uncleanness, or covetousness, let it not be once named among you, as becometh saints; Neither filthiness, nor foolish talking, nor jesting, which are not convenient: but rather giving of thanks. For this ye know, that no whoremonger, nor unclean person, nor covetous man, who is an idolater, hath any inheritance in the kingdom of Christ and of God. Let no man deceive you with vain words: for because of these things cometh the wrath of God upon the children of disobedience. Be not ye therefore partakers with them.*" Ephesians 5:3–7

"Flee also youthful lusts: but follow righteousness, faith, charity, peace, with them that call on the Lord out of a pure heart. 2 Timothy 2:22.

11. The Path Of Ingratitude:

"Because that, when they knew God, they glorified him not as God, neither were thankful; but became vain in their imaginations, and their foolish heart was darkened. Professing themselves to be wise, they became fools, And changed the glory of the uncorruptible God into an image made like to corruptible man, and to birds, and fourfooted beasts, and creeping things. Wherefore God also gave them up to uncleanness through the lusts of their own hearts, to dishonour their own bodies between themselves: Who changed the truth of God into a lie, and worshipped and served the creature more than the Creator, who is blessed for ever. Amen. For this cause God gave them up unto vile affections: for even their women did change the natural use into that which is against nature: And likewise also the men, leaving the natural use of the woman, burned in their lust one toward another; men with men working that which is unseemly, and receiving in themselves that recompence of their error which was meet. And even as they did not like to retain God in their knowledge, God gave them over to a reprobate mind, to do those things which are not convenient; Being filled with all unrighteousness, fornication, wickedness, covetousness, maliciousness; full of envy, murder, debate, deceit, malignity; whisperers, Backbiters, haters of God, despiteful, proud, boasters, inventors of evil things, disobedient to parents, Without understanding, covenantbreakers, without natural affection, implacable, unmerciful: Who knowing the judgment of God, that they which commit such things are worthy of death, not only do the same, but have pleasure in them that do them." Rom 1:21-32.

Whoever is not grateful is a great fool and will fall and sooner or later be grounded.

12. The Path That Ignores The Holy Spirit.
"But a certain man named Ananias, with Sapphira his wife, sold a possession, And kept back part of the price, his wife also being privy

to it, and brought a certain part, and laid it at the apostles' feet. But Peter said, Ananias, why hath Satan filled thine heart to lie to the Holy Ghost, and to keep back part of the price of the land? Whiles it remained, was it not thine own? and after it was sold, was it not in thine own power? why hast thou conceived this thing in thine heart? thou hast not lied unto men, but unto God. And Ananias hearing these words fell down, and gave up the ghost: and great fear came on all them that heard these things. And the young men arose, wound him up, and carried him out, and buried him. And it was about the space of three hours after, when his wife, not knowing what was done, came in. And Peter answered unto her, Tell me whether ye sold the land for so much? And she said, Yea, for so much. Then Peter said unto her, How is it that ye have agreed together to tempt the Spirit of the Lord? behold, the feet of them which have buried thy husband are at the door, and shall carry thee out. Then fell she down straightway at his feet, and yielded up the ghost: and the young men came in, and found her dead, and, carrying herforth, buried her by her husband. And great fear came upon all the church, and upon as many as heard these things." Acts 5:1-11.

When The Holy Spirit departs, glory departs.

13. The Path Of Impatience: Saul could not wait for Samuel to arrive. Faith and patience go together.

"That ye be not slothful, but be followers of them who through faith and patience inherit the promise" Heb 6:12.

"For ye have need of patience after that you have done the will of God, ye might receive the promise" Heb 10:36.

"Therefore thus saith the Lord GOD, Behold, I lay in Zion for a foundation a stone, a tried stone, a precious corner stone, a sure foundation: he that believeth shall not make haste." Isaiah 28:16

"Knowing this, that the trying of your faith worketh patience. But let patience have her perfect work, that ye may be perfect and entire, wanting nothing." James 1:3-4

He that believeth shall not make haste.

14. The Path Of Indiscipline.

"A man without self-control is as defenseless as a city with broken-down walls" Proverbs 25:28 (TLB).

15. The Path Of Pride.

"A man's pride shall bring him low: but honour shall uphold the humble in spirit." Prov. 29:23

"Then Uzziah was wroth, and had a censer in his hand to burn incense: and while he was wroth with the priests, the leprosy even rose up in his forehead before the priests in the house of the LORD, from beside the incense altar. And Azariah the chief priest, and all the priests, looked upon him, and, behold, he was leprous in his forehead, and they thrust him out from thence; yea, himself hasted also to go out, because the LORD had smitten him. And Uzziah the king was a leper unto the day of his death, and dwelt in a several house, being a leper; for he was cut off from the house of the LORD: and Jotham his son was over the king's house, judging the people of the land." 2 Chron 26:19-21.

King Uzziah was one man in history who learnt in a hard way that Pride is a killer. His Sin of pride eclipsed his success. Uzziah lived the last 10 years of his life Afflicted and Alienated; Removed, Relegated and Replaced as a result of the sin of pride.

16. The Path Of Unbelief

"And Samuel said, What hast thou done? And Saul said, Because I saw that the people were scattered from me, and that thou camest not within the days appointed, and that the Philistines gathered themselves together at Michmash; 1 Sam 13:11

"But without faith it is impossible to please him: for he that cometh to God must believe that he is, and that he is a rewarder of them that diligently seek him." Heb 11:6

Samuel said What has thou done? Saul said because "I saw". Saul started walking by sight and not by faith. Only Jonathan stepped out in faith.

"And Jonathan smote the garrison of the Philistines that was in Geba, and the Philistines heard of it. And Saul blew the trumpet throughout all the land, saying, Let the Hebrews hear. And all Israel heard say that Saul had smitten a garrison of the Philistines, and that Israel also was had in abomination with the Philistines. And the people were called together after Saul to Gilgal. And the Philistines gathered themselves together to fight with Israel, thirty thousand chariots, and six thousand horsemen, and people as the sand which is on the sea shore in multitude: and they came up, and pitched in Michmash, eastward from Bethaven." 1 Sam 13:3-5.

17. The Path Of Ungodliness.

"The ungodly are not so: but are like the chaff which the wind driveth away. Therefore the ungodly shall not stand in the judgment, nor sinners in the congregation of the righteous. For the LORD knoweth the way of the righteous: but the way of the ungodly shall perish." Psalms 1:4-6.

The Ungodly Is:
☐ Corrupted Extensively. Psalms 1:4
☐ Confounded Expediently. Psalms 1:5
☐ Condemned Eternally. Psalms 1:6

-The righteous will prosper.
-The wicked will perish.

The Ungodly lives a devilish, deceptive, distrustful destructive and deranged life on earth before ending up in hell.

18. The Path Of wickedness: The quality or state of being evil and mischievous. Wickedness is sinfulness. Leaders must develop the divine awareness that sustained Joseph: "How then can I do this great wickedness and sin against God?" (Gen. 39:9).

19.   The Resistance To Change.
Example is Apostle Peter. Acts 10:9-22. If you don't like divine change, you will sooner or later change position or be replaced.

IN CONCLUSION; TO AVOID THESE PATHS, LEADERS MUST FOLLOW 1 Tim 4:1-16.

"Now the Spirit speaketh expressly, that in the latter times some shall depart from the faith, giving heed to seducing spirits, and doctrines of devils; Speaking lies in hypocrisy; having their conscience seared with a hot iron; Forbidding to marry, and commanding to abstain from meats, which God hath created to be received with thanksgiving of them which believe and know the truth. For every creature of God is good, and nothing to be refused, if it be received with thanksgiving: For it is sanctified by the word of God and prayer. If thou put the brethren in remembrance of these things, thou shalt be a good minister of Jesus Christ, nourished up in the words of faith and of good doctrine, whereunto thou hast attained. But refuse profane and old wives' fables, and exercise thyself ratherunto godliness. For bodily exercise profiteth little: but godliness is profitable unto all things, having promise of the life that now is, and of that which is to come. This is a faithful saying and worthy of all acceptation. For therefore we both labour and suffer reproach, because we trust in the living God, who is the Saviour of all men, specially of those that believe. These things command and teach. Let no man despise thy youth; but be thou an example of the believers, in word, in conversation, in charity, in spirit, in faith, in purity. Till I come, give attendance to reading, to exhortation, to doctrine. Neglect not the gift that is in thee, which was given thee by prophecy, with the laying on of the hands of the presbytery. Meditate upon these things; give thyself wholly to them; that thy profiting may appear to all. Take heed unto thyself, and unto the doctrine; continue in them: for in doing this thou shalt both save thyself, and them that hear thee."

This chapter deals with the life and labors of ministry...Good Ministry - 1 Tm.4:1-6; Godly Ministry - 1 Tm.4:7-12; Growing Ministry - 1 Tm.4:13-16.

The foundations for successful spiritual leadership are:
A. Christ - linked Conversion. Acts 4:12; 16:31; Jn 3:17; 10:9; 1 Tm.4:6, 12; 2 Cor 5:17.

B. Christ-like Conversation. 1 Tm.4:12b; Prov.18:21; Eph.4:15; Ja.1:26; Prov.13:3a; Col.4:6

C. Christ-like Conduct. 1 Tm.4:12c; Phil.1:27; 1 Pt.1:15-16

D. Christ-like Compassion. 1 Tm.4:12d; 1 Jn 15:13.

E. Christ-like Confidence. 1 Tm.4:12e; 1 Jn 4:4.

F. Christ-like Conviction. 1 Tm.4:12f; Heb 11:6; 12:2a.

G. Christ-like Chastity. 1 Tm.4:12g; 2 Tim 2:22; Rom 12:1; Ps 139:14; Prov 31:10; 1 Cor.7:7, 9

Relish in the Word of God: 1 Tim.4:13.
a. Study 1 Tm.4:13a; 2 Tim 2:15

b. Share 1 Tm.4:13b-c

CONCLUSION: You can never lead beyond your leadership capacity. The world is looking for Limitless Leaders. You need to grow your capacity to be Limitless in order to be indispensable. The good news is that you can grow your capacity.

You grow your capacity through: FAITHFULNESS; FUNCTIONALITY; FOCUS; FRUITFULNESS & FORTITUDE.

Also Pray that God will enable you by His Grace to increase capacity on all fronts. There are good things waiting for you. You can be a Limitless leader. God has all you require to be Limitless in life.

OTHER BOOKS BY THE AUTHOR

1. Winning Habits
2. Achieving Success with Gods Winning Principles
3. Provoking High Favour
4. Advancing Through Adversity
5. Prosperity Principles
6. Overcoming the Problems of Life
7. 123 Nuggets for Great Achievements
8. Living Above Limitations
9. Poverty is too Expensive
10. Making Your Life Beautiful
11. The Money Question
12. From Tears to Cheers
13. Keys to Total Recovery
14. Achieving Excellence in Life
15. Overcoming Delays
16. Operating with the Right Speed
17. Divine Secrets
18. Irresistible Leader
19. From Expectation to Manifestation
20. Life Lessons from the Ants
21. Limitless Leadership

ACKNOWLEDGEMENT

I wish to acknowledge and appreciate the Almighty God for the privilege of been called to be a minister of the gospel of our Lord and Saviour Jesus Christ. It is the inspiration and insights of the Holy Spirit, that makes these outlines possible. All the glory belongs to Him.

I heartily thank my dear and highly supportive wife, Pastor Mrs Adesola Abosede Amenkhienan whose support on the home front and partnership in my ministerial activities provide the impetus for my dreams and achievements of which the latest is this book. You create a peaceful atmosphere around me that allows me focus and thrive. You are truly a gift from God.

My spiritual parents, Pastor E.A. Adeboye and Pastor Mrs. Folu Adeboye, have been of immeasurable value to my ministry. Their godly Leadership example and continuous encouragement for me to be my best in the work of the ministry has been a major impetus to keep striving to be better, for this I am very grateful.

To Pastor J. F. Odesola I say thanks for the encouragement. I must not forget the great contributions of Pastor A. A. Tugbobo and Pastor Alex Igbineweka to this work. The Lord will reward you mightily in Jesus name.

I profoundly appreciate the painstaking effort of Pastor Sesan Banjo and the Kenyan office team of Joshua Amenkhienan, Sylvia and Dennis who put the jigsaw materials together into a form ready for the next stage of the production You did a nice job.

BOOKS BY THIS AUTHOR

Strategic Living: Discover The Golden Keys To Living Well And Finishing Well

A book foreword by Dr. Myles Munroe, this book shows you the right ways to strategically position
yourself

Life Lessons From The Ants

In the book of the life lessons from the Ants, the writer describes how God is speaking to the
sluggard-this refers to one who is lazy, idle, careless, sticks to nothing, minds no business and brings
nothing to pass.

Irresistible Leader

IRRESISTIBLE LEADER, a book that would show you what it takes to become irresistible, lead irresistibly,
living a high definition life, principles from jesus' life, principles of leading irresistibly and many
more

The Money Question: The Christian And Money

The Money Question.This book helps dismiss the fact and mystery about money and Christianity. Most
Christians have related Christianity to poverty and riches to covetousness; but to the contrary Jesus
uses money as a symbol to explaining a lot of fact and figures about "heaven and earth" and
"relationship between the heavenly father and us".If we are called

Priest and Kings, meaning we are here
to reign and also worship HIM, we as kings are not to be poor in spirit, health and physical things.The
money question also shades more light on how to perceive money and relate it to your Christian faith.

Winning Habits: Another Bestseller From The Author Of Achieving Success

Winning Habits is a book that is meant to teach us how to succeed and be perpetual winners.

123 Nuggets For Great Achievements: From The Author Of Winning Habits

In 123 Nuggets for Great Achievements, bestselling author, Peter Amenkhienan has again capture truth
that will inspire you to leave above average, act your best and be your best in all that you do. Every
page is loaded with nuggets of wisdom, packaged to make the simple wise and even wiser.Consider
these:·It is the leading of God that makes you a progressive leader on earth·Dominion is impossible
without wisdom·The courage to take risk is the key to success·If your treasures are exposed to the
enemy, captivity is inevitable·You need a big mouth to control a big territory ·If you refuse to die, no
man will bury you·No one will befriend you if you have nothing to offer

Limitless Leadership

Limitless leadership

www.ingramcontent.com/pod-product-compliance
Lightning Source LLC
Chambersburg PA
CBHW071113220526
45467CB00004B/1852